God is Love

MORE THAN A FEELING

Latonya Sterling

God is Love
More Than a Feeling
By Latonya Sterling

Copyright © 2025 Latonya LSimmons Sterling
All rights reserved.

No part of this book may be reproduced, stored in a retrieval system, or transmitted in any form or by any means—electronic, mechanical, photocopying, recording, or otherwise—without the prior written permission of the publisher, except in the case of brief quotations embodied in critical articles or reviews.

Unless otherwise noted, all Scripture quotations are taken from the *Holy Bible, New International Version*®, NIV®. Copyright ©1973, 1978, 1984, 2011 by Biblica, Inc.™ Used by permission. All rights reserved worldwide.

ISBN: 9798999589705

First Edition

Cover design generated ChatGPT

Published by Latonya LSimmons Sterling

Contact: latonyasterling@gmail.com

Printed in the United States of America

In loving memory of my father, Eugene Johnson, Sr.

When you met Mom, she was already pregnant with me, but you claimed me as your own. You never once treated me like a stepdaughter. In fact, had you not told me yourself that you weren't my biological father, I would never have suspected it. All I ever knew was a father's love.

Thank you for showing me what unconditional love looks like. Though you are no longer here, your love continues to impact my life and reminds me daily of the love of my Heavenly Father. I thank God for blessing me with you.

" And so we know and rely on the love God has for us, God is love …."

1 John 4:16 (NIV)

Father God,

As this reader opens the pages of this book, I pray that their heart would open even wider to the truth of who You are—because You are love. Not a fleeting emotion or a shallow feeling, but the very essence of love itself. Let every word written here point back to You, the source of all love—pure, faithful, unconditional, and eternal.

Lord, reveal to them how deeply and personally You love them. Silence every voice of doubt, shame, or rejection, and let Your voice speak louder than them all: "You are My beloved." May they not just read about Your love, but experience it—feel it healing their hearts, restoring their identity, and renewing their mind.

And as they come to know Your love more deeply, may that love overflow. Teach them how to walk in love—in their families, friendships, workplaces, churches, and even with strangers. Let them become vessels through which Your love is seen, known, and felt in a world desperate for something real.

Let this journey through these pages not just be informative, but transformational. Let it draw them into intimacy with You, where love becomes more than a word or an idea—but a way of living. In Jesus' name, amen

Table of Contents

Introduction	1
Chapter 1 – Love: Beyond Human Understanding	3
Chapter 2 – Knowing God's Love for Yourself	9
Chapter 3 – Releasing God's Love Through Obedience and to Others	15
Chapter 4 – Love and Friendship	19
Chapter 5 – Love and Dating	23
Chapter 6 – Love in Marriage: Reflecting Christ and the Church	27
Chapter 7 – Love in Parenting: Raising Children in the Love the God	35
Chapter 8 – Love in Ministry: Serving With A Right Heart	37
Chapter 9 – Love in the Workplace	43
Chapter 10 – Love and Leadership	51
Chapter 11 – Love that Corrects	55
Final Word: The Love That Never Ends	59
Closing Prayer	61
Works Cited	63

Preface

Love. It's a word we hear every day, tossed around casually and often misunderstood. We say we love food, love our friends, love our spouse, or love a good movie. But what is love, really? This book is not about emotional fluff or poetic expressions. It's about a truth so foundational and life-altering that everything in your life hinges on it: **God is love.**

For years, I lived my life trying to love Father the best I knew how, trying to prove myself, trying to measure up. I didn't realize that I could never truly demonstrate His love to Him or anyone else fully until I received His love for me first. I pray that as you read these chapters, your heart will be opened to the unshakable, immeasurable love of Father, and that it will transform how you see yourself, how you see others, and how you live each day. Because love is not just a feeling. **Love is God Himself.**

Introduction

I remember years ago when I was going through new member's class at the first ministry I had ever joined. The class lasted about six months and focused on foundational principles of being a believer. At the end, we went through what they called "confirmation," where someone would speak prophetically over each person to affirm their journey and encourage them spiritually. Most people would fast before confirmation so they could prepare their hearts and minds to receive whatever God wanted to speak to them. That wasn't so with me.

At that time, I was still very immature in my walk. I hardly understood anything beyond those basic principles. Nevertheless, during confirmation, we all lined up in front of the church while everyone in the congregation watched and prayed as witnesses. The prophet came down the line, speaking powerful words over each person. Most people had their eyes closed and hands lifted, worshiping God deeply. I took the same *physical* posture, but I was not worshipping. I was listening closely to what he said to everyone else. Each word seemed so strong and life changing.

I thought to myself, *"When he gets to me, he's going to say something amazing—at least I hope he will."* When he reached me, he went silent for a moment. Then he simply said, *"Father, let your daughter know that You love her,"* and moved on to the next person.

In my mind, I thought, *"Seriously? What kind of word is that? God loves all of us. That's nothing special."* I was so disappointed that I got what I considered such a "low" word, that to bring attention to myself, I cried hysterically and fell out on the floor like I was slain in the Spirit. Yes, very pathetic.

Little did I know that was the exact word I needed. That was the word that would change my life forever. At the time, I didn't understand its value. But looking back, there was no greater word that could have been spoken over me than that. Father wanted me to know His love *personally*. In time, I would come to understand just how powerful those simple words were: *"God loves you."*

As you read these pages, I want you to know that what I share comes from my own journey of learning and applying God's love in everyday life. God has graciously revealed truths to me that I once did not understand, and He has shown me how His love transforms parenting, friendships, leadership, and even personal struggles. At the same time, I realize that God's love, while the same in its essence, may be expressed in different ways in each of our lives. The way He has led me may not look exactly like the way He leads you. My prayer is that as you read, you will not feel confined to my experiences but encouraged to discover how God desires for His love to be lived out uniquely through you.

Chapter 1

Love: Beyond Human Understanding

For centuries, people have tried to define love, categorize it, and explain it. Philosophers, poets, and cultures across history have all attempted to put words around something that feels deeply important yet difficult to explain. Often, love is treated as something abstract; something meaningful but unclear, powerful but unstable.

The word abstract describes something that exists as an idea or a concept but not in a clear or practical way. This is often how love is treated. People talk about love constantly, yet when asked to define it or live it out consistently, confusion follows. Love becomes something everyone references but few can clearly explain or practice with stability.

The ancient Greeks attempted to categorize love into different forms. They used words to describe romantic attraction (eros), friendship (phileo), family affection (storge), and other human experiences. These categories were developed by philosophers such as Plato and Aristotle, who lived centuries before Christ and did not know or serve the God of Israel. Their thinking was rooted in human reason and Greek mythology, not divine revelation. While their ideas influenced Western thought, they did not reveal the true nature of love as Scripture reveals it.

Notably, while these Greek categories are often taught today, they do not appear in the New Testament as philosophical explanations of love. Scripture does not present love as a theory or a category. Instead, it presents love as a person. *God is Love.*

While the ancient Greeks used several words to describe human experiences of affection, the New Testament writers used one primary word to describe God's love: *agapē*. This word did not originate as a philosophical category created by Plato or Aristotle, nor was it developed to explain romantic, familial, or emotional bonds. In Scripture, *agapē* is used to describe the self-giving, faithful love that comes from God Himself. Over time, the Church began using the term *agapē* to help distinguish God's love from human affection. However, the word itself is not the source of love, nor does it define God. Scripture does not teach us to understand love through a Greek term; it teaches us to know love by knowing God. *Agapē* is simply the word Scripture uses to point to a reality that already exists: God is love. The focus is not the term, but the Person the term describes.

The Word of God tells us plainly: "Whoever does not love does not know God, because God is love" (1 John 4:8, NIV). This statement is not poetic language. It is a direct revelation. God does not merely have love. God does not fall in love. *God is love.* That means love is not something God feels—it is who He is. Love is not an emotion God experiences; it is His very nature.

This truth immediately challenges the way we commonly speak about love. We use phrases like "I'm in love," "I fell in love," or "we fell out of love." These expressions make love sound accidental and unstable—something we stumble into and slip out of without intention. If love works that way, then it is dependent on feelings. And feelings change. But God's love does not fluctuate. It does not depend on mood, excitement, or convenience. It is steady, intentional, faithful, and governed by His character. If God is love, then love cannot be reduced to emotion. Love must be something lived, not merely felt.

This abstract view of love also shapes the questions people often ask, such as, "Do you love God?" or "How much do you love God?" These questions assume love is something we measure or perform. When love is viewed this way, the focus subtly shifts from God to us.

Scripture points in a different direction. Love does not begin with our effort. "We love because He first loved us" (1 John 4:19). Love starts with God's initiative, not our obedience. God is not asking us to generate love from ourselves. He supplies what He invites us to live from. Romans 5:5 tells us that God's love has already been poured into our hearts through the Holy Spirit. In other words, God is not saying, "Try harder to love." He is saying, "Live from the love I have already given you."

Because love comes from God, it is not indiscriminate or reckless. God's love is kind, but it is also wise. It is patient, but it is also truthful. Scripture describes love as patient, kind, not self-seeking, not easily angered, truthful, faithful, restrained, and enduring (1 Corinthians 13:4–7). These are not emotions. They are expressions of

God's character. This is why love is not proven by intensity, attraction, or emotional closeness alone. Love is revealed through action shaped by wisdom. Love shows up in how we treat people, how we speak, how we choose faithfulness, and how we respond when feelings fluctuate.

We see the clearest picture of love in Jesus Himself. Scripture tells us that Jesus is the image of the invisible God (Colossians 1:15). Jesus said, "Whoever has seen Me has seen the Father" (John 14:9). He explained that He only did what He saw His Father doing and only spoke what His Father commanded (John 5:19; John 12:49). Through Jesus, love became visible. Love took on flesh.

God's love has always been steady, even when His people were not. Israel turned away repeatedly, yet God remained faithful, calling them back with mercy. "I have loved you with an everlasting love; I have drawn you with unfailing kindness" (Jeremiah 31:3, NIV). This enduring love was never permission to continue in sin; it was always an invitation to return.

Understanding love this way changes everything. Dating becomes less about chasing feelings and more about demonstrating character. Marriage becomes less about constant emotional excitement and more about faithfulness, patience, and commitment. Relationships become more stable because love is no longer something we fear losing. It becomes something we practice.

Love looks like listening instead of reacting. Keeping your word. Choosing kindness when it would be easier to withdraw. Setting healthy boundaries. Remaining present when things are difficult. Love is not blind, irrational, or uncontrolled. God is not blind. God is not irrational. And because God is love, love reflects His clarity and wisdom.

Most importantly, no person is meant to be the source of love. God alone is love. When you know you are already loved by Him, you are free to love others without demanding that they complete you, validate you, or make you whole. Love becomes something you give, not something you chase.

Love is not an idea.
Love is not a feeling.
Love is not a concept.

Love is a person. And that person is God.

Father, thank You for revealing to me that You are love. Thank You for showing me that Your love is not based on my performance, but on Your unchanging nature. Help me to rest in that truth, receive it fully, and reflect it in every area of my life. I am grateful that Your love is constant, faithful, and true. In Jesus' name, amen.

Latonya Sterling

Chapter 2

Knowing God's Love for Yourself

When I think back to that prophetic word spoken over me – "Father, let your daughter know that You love her" – I realize now it was the most powerful word I could have ever received. But at the time, I didn't understand it. I was shallow and thought I would get a word of doing something great. I didn't know what it meant to truly know God's love for myself. I knew God loved people. I knew John 3:16 said, "For God so loved the world..." But I didn't know that God loved *me* personally, deeply, unconditionally, and unchangingly.

Some of us often live with a general concept of God's love. We believe He loves the world, but we don't live as if He loves us individually. Yet scripture makes it clear in 1 John 4:10 that, "This is love: not that we loved God, but that he loved us and sent his Son as an atoning sacrifice for our sins." God's love isn't proven by how passionately we worship Him, how fervently we pray, or how diligently we serve. God's love was proven on the cross. Before you ever lifted your hands in worship, before you ever prayed, before you were even born, God set His love upon you. That is why the apostle Paul prayed, "...that Christ may dwell in your hearts through faith. And I pray that you, being rooted and established in love, may have power...to grasp how wide and long and high and deep is the love of Christ, and to know this love that surpasses knowledge." – Ephesians 3:17–19 (NIV)

Paul understood that unless we are rooted and established in God's love, we will be unstable in every other area of life. We will serve out of obligation instead of joy. We will live to earn approval instead of resting in acceptance. We will obey to avoid punishment rather than out of a place of love. But when you know God's love for yourself, everything changes.

Knowing God's love is not about head knowledge. It is about experiential revelation. The Greek word for "know" in Ephesians 3:19 is *ginóskó*, which means to know by intimate experience. God doesn't want you to just read about His love. He wants you to encounter it. He wants you to be so rooted in it that nothing can shake you. God's love is unearned. Romans 5:8 says, "But God demonstrates his own love for us in this: While we were still sinners, Christ died for us." While we were still broken, stubborn, rebellious, and prideful, Jesus laid down His life for us. We weren't even born when He did that for us. That means His love is not based on our goodness but His goodness. We cannot make Him love us more by praying harder or serving more. We cannot make Him love us less by failing. His love is constant because it flows out of who He is.

While I didn't connect the dots to God's love in my youth, I learned early what the love of a father looked like—not because I had the perfect family situation, but because I had a faithful father in Eugene Johnson, Sr. I grew up under his roof, ate his food, and was shaped by both his love and discipline. I absolutely adored my daddy.

Though he had his own struggles rooted in a difficult childhood, he was mine—and no one could tell me otherwise.

I still remember being in junior high when he told me something I hadn't expected: he wasn't my biological father. He explained that he had met my biological dad, who had asked him to take care of me. I later found out that the reason my dad chose to tell me at that time was because we had recently been at a family gathering where all of us kids were bragging about our dads. I was so proud of mine that I had a lot to say. Apparently, one of the kids blurted out, "He's not your daddy!" I didn't hear it, but someone else did—and that someone told my mother, which prompted my parents to finally have the conversation with me. But even in that moment, I didn't feel abandoned or confused. All I could think about was getting back outside to play with my friends. I looked at him and said, "It's okay, Dad. You're my dad. Can I go back outside now?" I hugged him and ran off, unaffected—because nothing had been missing from my life. Love had already been present, day in and day out. DNA didn't define my fatherhood experience—love did.

I remember one time when my mom and I had a disagreement that left me in tears. I was sitting outside on the front steps when my dad came out, sat beside me, gently placed his hand on my shoulder and said, "Tonya, I don't have a lot to give, but if you ever need me, I'm here." That moment stayed with me. And when I finally moved away from home, he said, "Tonya, I'm not putting you out, so if you can't make it out there, you know you can come back home anytime you want." It was moments like these that I undeniably knew my daddy loved me—and it wasn't because of anything I had done, but simply because of who he was. That's how our Heavenly Father is.

Later in life, I desired to meet my biological father, not from lack, but out of compassion and the hope that he would come to know Jesus. Unfortunately, I never got the opportunity to meet my biological father, James Key. But, I never felt I lacked a father. My dad, who just passed on May 17, 2025, loved me as if I had come from his very own blood. And I believe that was the love of my Heavenly Father expressed through my earthly one. It taught me—before I could even fully understand it—that God's love isn't distant or theoretical. It's present. It's consistent. It shows up.

When you truly know God's love for yourself, it changes how you live. You stop striving to be accepted because you understand that you are already accepted in the Beloved (Ephesians 1:6). You no longer fear rejection, because perfect love casts out fear (1 John 4:18). And you stop seeking validation from people, because you are secure in the unwavering affection of your Heavenly Father.

Knowing God's love for yourself is absolutely imperative for your entire spiritual life. Everything flows from it. When you know His love, you can finally love Him freely. You can love others without needing something in return. You can obey Him with joy, knowing that obedience is simply an expression of love rather than a means to earn His approval.

God is Love

My prayer is that you will experience the height, depth, width, and length of His love in a way that transforms you from the inside out. Because only then can you truly live the life God has called you to live.

Father, thank You for loving me. Thank You for seeing me, choosing me, and calling me Your own. Your love is more than I could ever earn, yet You give it freely. I'm grateful that Your love never changes—even when I do. Help me to receive it fully, walk in it daily, and reflect it in every part of my life. I love You, because You first loved me. In Jesus' name, amen.

Latonya Sterling

Chapter 3

Releasing God's Love Through Obedience and to Others

Knowing God's love for yourself is the foundation of your walk with Him, but it doesn't stop there. God's love was never meant to remain bottled up within us. His love flows in so that it can flow out. The way we release God's love to others is through obedience to Him and through demonstrating that love in our relationships. Jesus said in John 14:15, "If you love me, keep my commands." This verse isn't about proving our love to God through rigid religious duty. Rather, it is a natural response. When you truly know God's love, obedience becomes a joy, not a burden. You trust His commands because you trust His heart. You know that everything He asks of you is motivated by His love for you.

The apostle John also wrote, "We love because He first loved us" (1 John 4:19). Our ability to love others—to forgive them, to show mercy, to be patient and kind—all of it flows out of the revelation that God first loved us. Without knowing His love, we will always try to love others from a place of emptiness, and eventually we grow bitter, weary, or resentful. But when we remain rooted in God's love, there is always an overflow. It causes us to think about how we can love others.

I experienced this personally when I was dating my husband before we got married. I couldn't automatically tell him that I loved him, even though he had no problem saying it to me. I knew love wasn't butterflies in my stomach. It wasn't him making me laugh or the fact that he could kiss well. I understood that love was so much more than that, and I couldn't say "I love you" just based on a feeling. I realized I had to make a decision. Loving him would mean consciously demonstrating the kind of love described in 1 Corinthians 13. I even had to teach my children that love isn't saying "I love you" in response to someone else's words. Love is making a deliberate, ongoing choice to act like God toward someone—to be patient, kind, forgiving, and selfless … no matter how they act.

Think about it this way: a dry sponge can't clean anything. But when a sponge is soaked and full, it naturally releases water as it touches other surfaces. In the same way, when we stay soaked in God's love, we naturally release it to everyone we come in contact with—not out of duty, but out of overflow.

Loving others is not an optional part of our faith—it's the natural evidence that we truly know God. 1 John 4:7–8 says, "Dear friends, let us love one another, for love comes from God. Everyone who loves has been born of God and knows God. Whoever does not love does not know God, because God is love." *When God commands us to love, He is not forcing us into something impossible or burdensome. He is inviting us to be toward others the way He has been toward us.* It's not about striving to be a "good person" by human effort; it's about surrendering to His love so that it can transform us from the inside out and flow freely to those around us. God knows we are capable of loving this way—not in our own strength, but because His love is alive and at work within us.

Sometimes, loving others means forgiving someone who hurt you. Other times, it's serving someone who doesn't acknowledge or appreciate it. It might even be courageously sharing the truth of the gospel with someone God places in your path. No matter what form it takes, real love is always active. As 1 John 3:18 reminds us, "Dear children, let us not love with words or speech but with actions and in truth." This kind of love isn't just what God asks of us—it's what He has already given us the power to live out.

If you truly know God's love, it will show. People will feel it in your words, see it in your attitude, and experience it through your actions. This doesn't mean you will be perfect. It means that even when you fall short, you will return to the One who is perfect love and allow Him to continue transforming you.

As you continue this journey of understanding that God is love, remember: You cannot pour out what you do not possess. Make it your priority to consistently sit in God's presence, meditate on His Word, and receive His love afresh. Then, go into your world, your home, your church, your workplace—and let that love overflow into every relationship and situation you face. Because real love is not that we love Him, but that He loves us. And when you live from that place, obedience becomes worship, and loving others becomes a natural outpouring of His love within you.

Father, thank You for Your unfailing love toward me. Thank You for helping me to demonstrate that love to others. Help me to obey Your command to love—not out of obligation, but as a response to the love You have poured into my heart. Teach me to act with kindness, patience, and grace, reflecting Your love in everything I do. In Jesus' name, amen.

Chapter 4

Love and Friendships

Friendship is one of life's greatest blessings. The Bible calls us to love one another deeply (1 Peter 1:22), and that love is so tangible in the relationships we build with friends. But friendship, like all relationships, requires effort, vulnerability, and above all, love that reflects God's heart. I think about some of the friendships that have shaped me—some that challenged me, others that carried me, and some that taught me how to truly love others.

Years ago, I served alongside a wonderful woman named Rhonda Mitchell in children's ministry. Rhonda was a faithful, trusted friend, but I did not know how to be a good friend in return. I would often say to Rhonda, *"If you need anything, let me know,"* but deep down, I hoped she would never ask. I was disingenuous, keeping my own walls up, afraid to truly engage and support. Yet, Rhonda continued to show up faithfully, loving me despite my shortcomings. When she moved away, I realized how much I had learned from her steadfastness. Thanks be to God for the love working in her heart, because without that love, our friendship might not have lasted.

Then there is my sister in Christ, Lisa Evans—a strong woman of God and a friend every woman needs. Lisa's love is real, authentic, and fierce. In my baby years as a believer she helped me to grow in gifts and talents I didn't even realize I had. She didn't try to fix me, but something about her faith and strength made me want to rise higher. Her walk with God stirred something in me—and that was accountability in its purest form. When life gets tough, Lisa's words echo in my heart: *"Press on,"* reminding me to keep moving forward no matter what, trusting that God is with me every step of the way. Her quick wit and humor made the journey lighter, but it's her genuine love that has kept our friendship strong even through distance and time.

One of the most challenging friendships I experienced was with a young woman whose name I won't mention for the sake of her privacy. When I met her, she was carrying heavy trauma. I became deeply involved in her life, but I was too immature to minister to her effectively. The weight of her struggles began to wear me down. Yet, as I grew in the Lord and God's love expanded in me, I learned to love her the way she needed—not with judgment or frustration, but with patience and grace. Even when she was offended by me or withdrew, I remained steadfast, understanding that her pain was not about me personally. I was not a doormat; I simply chose to love her through the hard seasons, ready to receive her back whenever she returned. That kind of love reflects how our Father loves us—patiently, graciously, and unconditionally.

Family friendships are just as precious to me. My mother, sister, and brothers are my closest friends, and we prioritize peace and unity above all. I refuse to let disagreements or arguments come between us. If I must apologize first, I will, because the love of God will not allow me to remain separated from those closest to me. Just as nothing can separate us from the love of God (Romans 8:38-39), His love binds us together—even when we are messy and imperfect.

In a society when many women lament about not having trusted female friends, I am also blessed with wonderful sisters in Christ. There is something special about a group of women who love one another deeply, who speak truth and encouragement freely, and who hold each other accountable in love. We connect outside structured settings, we fellowship often, and our hearts are knitted together in a unique and intimate way.

True friendship reflects God's love in powerful ways. It shows up as faithfulness, staying through thick and thin, just as God never abandons us. It includes honesty, speaking the truth in love—even when it's hard to hear. Forgiveness plays a vital role, letting go of offenses and refusing to hold grudges. True friends offer support, helping to carry one another's burdens and celebrating victories together. They bring encouragement, building each other up to fulfill God's purposes. And they provide accountability, lovingly guiding one another back when they begin to stray. In all of this, godly friendship becomes a living expression of God's heart.

Friendship is a mirror of the relationship God desires with us—intimate, honest, and unconditional. Jesus called His disciples friends (John 15:15) and showed us how to love sacrificially. In friendships, God teaches us to love beyond convenience, beyond feelings, and even beyond seasons of difficulty. Love chooses to stay when it's easier to walk away. Love reaches out when the other is distant. Love forgives when it is easier to be offended.

If we can learn to love our friends with God's love, our friendships become a living testimony of His grace and faithfulness. In a world that often feels isolating, these genuine bonds remind us that we are never alone. We belong—to God and to one another.

Father, thank You for the gift of friendship—within ministry, in my everyday life, and even among family members who have become true friends. I'm grateful for relationships that foster trust, support, and accountability. Thank You for teaching me how to be a friend, especially when my tendency is to focus on myself. Thank You for helping me not to be easily offended and for giving me the grace to reconcile when strife arises. Lord, You've shown me that friendship isn't just about having people to spend time with—it's an opportunity to value others the way You do. Help me to keep growing in love, humility, and grace in every relationship You've placed in my life. In Jesus' name, amen.

Chapter 5

Love and Dating

There's something special about young love—that season in life when emotions run high and hearts awaken to the joy of companionship. When we meet someone who makes us smile a little brighter and laugh a little louder, we often want to talk to them all the time, share every part of our day, and spend every possible moment together. That feeling is beautiful. It's natural. But as believers, we must understand that love is not just a feeling—it is a fruit of the Spirit, and it must be guided by truth, respect, and self-control.

Dating in Christ looks different from the way the world often portrays it. In the world, dating is often driven by physical attraction, impulse, and the pursuit of pleasure. But in the Kingdom of God, dating is not a game of trial and error; it's a purposeful journey toward either clarity or commitment. Love doesn't pressure—it protects. Love doesn't rush—it reflects. Love doesn't manipulate—it matures.

Love is not blind—it sees clearly. And when it is truly present in a dating relationship, it governs every aspect of it: the conversation, the behavior, the intentions, and the direction. The words we speak to one another in dating should build up, not break down. Are we speaking words of life, encouragement, and affirmation? Or are we speaking words laced with lust, flattery, or hidden agendas?

A dating relationship rooted in Christ will guard the heart (Proverbs 4:23) and honor the body (1 Corinthians 6:19-20). Love doesn't take what doesn't belong to it. Love gives, but it gives in a way that is pure and respectful. It gives time, patience, kindness, and care—but it does not take purity, joy, or peace in exchange. Love honors boundaries. It values the spiritual well-being of the other person above the momentary gratification of self.

The way we date reflects the way we love. Are we choosing places to go that support wise decisions and help us avoid temptation, or are we purposely putting ourselves in situations that test our restraint? Love asks that question. Love steers the relationship away from compromise and into places of safety, light, and accountability. A godly couple doesn't just ask, "How far is too far?" They ask, "How can we glorify God in our relationship?"

Accountability is key in a Christ-centered relationship, but it is often misunderstood. Accountability is not about telling everyone your business or living under constant scrutiny. It is about having at least one trusted, wise person—such as a mentor, pastor, parent, or spiritually grounded friend—who can see what you may not be able to see clearly. Feelings can sometimes cloud judgment, but love welcomes wisdom. Love is willing to receive perspective. Too often, couples date in secret or isolation, which can lead to confusion and compromise. Not because they are intentionally doing wrong, but because unchecked emotion can quietly blind discernment. Accountability brings light, not control. It creates space for clarity, protection, and truth. Love is not afraid of transparency, because love desires what is good, honest, and lasting.

In Scripture, one of the clearest examples of a love relationship marked by godliness and mutual respect is found in the story of Ruth and Boaz (Ruth 1–4). After tragedy left Ruth widowed and alone in a foreign land, she chose to stay with her mother-in-law Naomi and live a life of integrity and humility. Boaz, a noble and godly man, noticed Ruth—not just her beauty, but her character. He honored her, protected her, and never took advantage of her vulnerability. He didn't rush her or use her; he made sure she felt safe and covered.

Their relationship was not rushed or manipulated. It was marked by care, honor, and a deep respect for one another and for God. Boaz even ensured that everything was done legally and properly when he stepped in to redeem her. In the end, their relationship—rooted in godliness and love—led to a marriage that played a part in the lineage of Jesus Christ. That's what godly love can do.

When we allow love to govern our dating relationships, we create space for something beautiful to grow—something that has the potential to carry into a strong and lasting marriage. A marriage built on mutual respect, spiritual unity, and emotional safety doesn't just happen on the wedding day—it begins in the dating season.

I wish I could say I always lived this out perfectly, but I didn't. I failed in many of these areas when it came to dating. I ignored boundaries, didn't seek wise counsel, and allowed emotions to lead me instead of love guided by truth. As a result, I found myself in relationships that were not only unfruitful but also damaging. I brought emotional baggage and unnecessary struggles into my marriage—things God never intended for me to carry. But even in that, God met me with redemption. His grace covered my mistakes, and His love continues to teach me how to love rightly. I share this chapter not from a place of judgment, but from a place of hope. My prayer is that any single reader who picks up this book will learn from my failures and avoid the trappings of misguided feelings. May this truth guide you into something more—something holy, whole, and life-giving.

Love doesn't ignore red flags. Love doesn't pretend. Love doesn't sneak or manipulate. It walks in the light. It celebrates truth. It honors God. And when we learn to love well in dating, we are preparing ourselves—and the one we're dating—for a relationship that reflects the love of Christ and honors the heart of God.

Father, Thank You for the gift of love and the beauty of companionship. As I walk through this season of dating, help me to be guided not by fleeting emotions, but by Your truth, wisdom, and Spirit. Teach me to love in a way that protects, respects, and reflects Your heart. Guard my decisions, purify my intentions, and lead me away from compromise. May my relationships honor You, build me up, and prepare me for the kind of love that reflects Christ. Surround me with wise counsel, and give me the courage to walk in the light. I trust You with my heart, my future, and the love story You are writing for me. In Jesus' name, amen.

Chapter 6

Love in Marriage
Reflecting Christ and the Church

Marriage is one of the most powerful demonstrations of God's love on earth. It is not a social contract or a romantic partnership built on emotion. It is a divine covenant designed to reflect Christ's relationship with His Church. Scripture does not present marriage as two people trying to stay emotionally "in love," but as two people choosing to live out God's love toward one another in faithfulness and truth.

In Ephesians 5:25–27 (ESV), Paul writes, "Husbands, love your wives, as Christ loved the church and gave himself up for her, that he might sanctify her… so that he might present the church to himself in splendor, without spot or wrinkle or any such thing." This is a high calling. Husbands are commanded to love their wives the way Christ loves the Church—sacrificially, intentionally, and with a love that seeks her good, her growth, and her wholeness. Christ's love was not based on the Church's perfection, but on His own character. He loved us while we were still sinners and laid down His life to redeem and transform us.

Wives are also called to respond with respect and honor, submitting to their husbands as unto the Lord (Ephesians 5:22–24). This submission is not about inferiority or forced obedience. It is a willing response of trust that reflects the Church's relationship with Christ. In a healthy, godly marriage, both husband and wife are called to submit to one another in love (Ephesians 5:21), serving one another selflessly under the lordship of Christ.

Dad Dotson once taught me that if I learned to submit to the Father, I would naturally submit to my husband. Entrusting God to lead me as a wife means trusting that He will always lead me to act in love toward my husband. Many women struggle in this area because submission is approached horizontally first—focused on the husband's behavior—rather than vertically, rooted in obedience to God. When submission is disconnected from God, it often becomes reluctant, superficial, or resistant. Jesus submitted to the Father even when it led Him to the cross for a world full of flawed people. In the same way, I can submit to a perfect God while married to a flawed man—just as I myself am flawed. This is only possible through the Holy Spirit living and working within me.

Many marriages among born-again believers struggle, not because love is absent, but because love is misunderstood. God is love, and Christ is present in their midst, yet love is often missing in daily practice. Instead of sacrificial love, selfishness takes root. Instead of honor and respect, contempt grows. Instead of grace, harshness appears. This happens when love is treated as a feeling rather than a way of living. It is impossible to love your spouse the way God commands without first knowing and embracing God's love for yourself.

We truly need to understand that the Father loves us unconditionally. To say that God loves unconditionally means that His love is not initiated, sustained, or withdrawn based on human behavior, worthiness, or performance. When you receive His love, you no longer demand perfection from your spouse. You forgive more freely because you know how deeply you have been forgiven. You serve without resentment because you are secure in God's love, not dependent on your spouse to fill what only God can fill. Marriage was never meant to be about getting your needs met. It is about giving love faithfully and trusting God to meet your deepest needs. Your spouse will fail you at times, but when you are rooted in God's love, you can respond with grace, patience, and kindness, just as Christ does toward you daily.

This is where many people struggle with language. Phrases like "I'm in love with my husband" or "I fell in love" often center love in emotion. But biblical love is not rooted in how we feel; it is revealed in how we live. If God is love, then love is not something we fall into or out of—it is something we choose to express. Love is not an abstract idea or a passing feeling. Love is a lived posture shaped by God's character.

So rather than asking, "Am I in love?" a more truthful question is, "How am I choosing to love?" Love shows up in patience, honesty, faithfulness, restraint, and commitment. It is expressed through how we speak, how we forgive, how we remain present, and how we honor covenant even when emotions fluctuate. This does not mean affection or emotion is unimportant; it means emotion is not the authority.

This understanding brings clarity and stability to marriage. Love is no longer something you chase or fear losing. It becomes something you practice. You choose to love your spouse by how you treat them, not by how strongly you feel in every moment. Marriage becomes less about emotional intensity and more about covenant faithfulness.

The passage in 1 Corinthians 13:4–7, often read at weddings, is not poetic sentiment—it is a blueprint for how God's love is meant to function in marriage. Love is patient and kind. It is not self-seeking or easily angered. It keeps no record of wrongs. Imagine marriages where both husband and wife lived from this kind of love daily—not driven by mood or circumstance, but governed by the reality that God is love and He lives within them. Marriage is not about being happy every moment; it is about being formed—refined by God into people who reflect His heart.

Forgiveness is one of the clearest demonstrations of God's love. God showed His love by sending His only Son for the forgiveness of our sins. I remember praying for the state of the world and then being drawn to pray for repentance and forgiveness within the body of Christ. I realized that the world would recognize God and His people not by perfection, but by love and unity. During that time, the Lord began revealing resentments I had buried in my heart toward my husband over past hurts. Though I did not act unkindly outwardly, there was hidden turmoil within me. Responding with godly sorrow led me to repentance. I confessed honestly—to God and to my husband—and something shifted. From that day forward, I experienced freedom in my heart and a deeper capacity to love. This is what God's love does: it exposes what binds us so that we can be healed and transformed.

If you are married, ask God to deepen your understanding and confidence in His love so that you can pour it out onto your spouse. If you are single, ask Him to root you so firmly in His love that when marriage comes, you enter it not looking to be completed, but already whole—ready to give rather than demand. Marriage is not simply about two people loving each other. It is about two people becoming a living picture of the greatest love story ever told: Christ and His Church.

Father, thank You for the gift of love in my marriage. Thank You for giving me the grace to walk in forgiveness and the courage to submit to my spouse without fear. Help me to love not based on my spouse's behavior, but because Your love flows through me. Help me to continually grow in Your love, that I may reflect You faithfully every day. In Jesus' name, amen.

Latonya Sterling

Chapter 7

Love in Parenting
Raising Children in the Love of God

Parenting is one of the greatest responsibilities God entrusts to us. It is also one of the greatest opportunities to demonstrate His love in a practical, life-changing way. As parents, our children's first understanding of who God is often comes from how we treat them, correct them, and love them or fail to demonstrate love well.

One of the greatest lessons I have learned as a parent was that it is God's love working through me that truly shapes my children's hearts. When I first became a mother, I thought raising godly children meant enforcing strict religious routines and making sure they did everything "right." I didn't want them to just know about God—I wanted them to know Him deeply. In my early days, I believed that meant making them read the Bible daily, pray a certain way, and follow spiritual practices exactly as I did. However, this strict approach did not make my children love God. In fact, it caused some of them pull away. While they followed the rules in my house, it wasn't out of love or a genuine desire to know God—it was simply parent/child compliance. But God began to teach me something profound: His love doesn't *force* people into relationship—it invites them. His love is patient and kind. He showed me that my job as a parent was not to force my kids into *my routine*, but to create an atmosphere where they could *encounter Him for themselves*. That meant modeling Christ through how my husband and I lived, loved, forgave, and walked with God in everyday life.

Many of us train our children the way our parents trained us, thinking that it is the right way simply because it is all we know. But the truth is, *some* of the things we were taught were damaging. Perhaps it was harsh discipline without love, silence in place of affirmation, or religious rules without relationship. But, when Christ comes in, He comes to heal all of that. He shows us how to train up our children *His way* – with truth and grace, discipline and love, correction and compassion. He breaks generational cycles of fear and replaces them with His perfect love that casts out fear.

Another way God's love transformed my parenting was in the area of discipline. Because I loved my children so deeply, I wanted to discipline them in love – not in anger, frustration, or embarrassment. Proverbs 13:24 says, "Whoever spares the rod hates their children, but the one who loves them is careful to discipline them." God disciplines us because He loves us, *not because He is angry at us*. Discipline is meant to correct, protect, and restore – not to shame or belittle. The Lord taught me never to confuse who my children were with their behavior. Their behavior needed correction, but their identity as loved, valued children never changed. When I disciplined them, I learned to address what they did rather than labeling who they were. Instead of saying, *"You're so bad,"* I learned to say, *"What you did was wrong, and here's why. But I love you, and God loves you, and that never changes."* This way, they never felt that my love or God's love was conditional upon their behavior.

God has also shown me that some of the most powerful ministry in parenting happens in silence. I have learned that listening to my children's hearts matters more than reacting quickly to their behavior. When I slow down and truly hear them, I am better able to discern what is actually going on beneath the surface. I am not my children's boss; I have been entrusted with the privilege of stewarding their lives, guiding them with wisdom, patience, and love rather than control.

The love of God also taught me to recognize when I was wrong and to apologize to my children. There were times I disciplined too harshly or spoke out of anger. In those moments, the Holy Spirit would show me my heart, reminding me that humility before my children was just as important as teaching them humility before others. I would go to them and say, *"I was wrong. I shouldn't have spoken to you that way. Please forgive me."* At first, it felt uncomfortable. I worried it would make me look weak. But what it actually did was teach my children how to apologize. It showed them that even adults can be wrong, and that repentance is not shameful – it is honorable. It taught them that real love takes responsibility and seeks reconciliation. This is the kind of love we are called to demonstrate to our children. A love that protects them, corrects them in truth, builds them up, and shows them the character of God through our words and actions.

Parenting is not about raising perfect children. It is about raising children who know they are loved unconditionally by God and by us. It is about creating an atmosphere where they feel safe to grow, to make mistakes, to learn repentance, and to pursue God for themselves. At the end of the day, my greatest desire is not that my children simply follow rules, but that they *encounter the love of God* in such a real way that it transforms their hearts and lives forever. When they know God's love, they will walk in their identity, they will stand firm in their faith, and they will love others from a place of security – the same way God loves them.

I want to make it clear that what I've shared here is simply how God has led me in my parenting journey. Every family is different, and God may guide you in ways that look different from mine. These reflections are not the only way to raise children in God's love, but simply the lessons He has shown me along the way. My hope is that you will seek His direction for your own children and trust Him to give you wisdom that fits your home.

Father, thank You for teaching me how to demonstrate Your love to my children. Thank You for showing me that love is expressed not just in words, but in how I train them, encourage them, and even discipline them. Thank You for the grace to admit when I'm wrong and to model forgiveness through repentance. Help me to live a life before them that reflects Your heart and draws them closer to You. In Jesus' name, amen.

Chapter 8

Love in Ministry
Serving With a Right Heart

Ministry is not about titles, positions, or recognition—it's about love. Real ministry flows from the love of God within us, and that love always seeks to serve rather than to be served. It glorifies God and advances the Kingdom. Ministry is not a way to prove love for God; it is the result of being formed by His love. When love is understood as formation rather than obligation, service becomes an overflow instead of a performance.

My husband and I have been in ministry for as long as we've been together. We started by serving in the children's ministry at the church community where we met. He taught elementary school–aged kids, and I led the preschool and kindergarten area. It was work. It required prayer, preparation, and submission. And truthfully, it was only through the love of God that I was able to serve the way I did—especially during a time when I was wrestling with my own identity in Christ and learning to walk in freedom from religious rituals. I wasn't serving to prove my devotion to God; I was learning how to live from His love while serving others.

I was blessed to have amazing leaders who modeled what it means to serve with love. My mentors, Mom and Dad Dotson, were incredible examples of true servant leadership. When I served alongside them in the children's ministry, they were right there with us—sleeves rolled up, fully engaged. Many Sundays, I would spend time in their home. They truly became family. Even after a full day of serving at church, Mom would prepare dinner with joy. They were like second parents to me. Titles didn't matter to them—they simply loved God and genuinely loved His people. Before they moved on, they made sure we were trained not just in tasks, but in heart—to love both God and the children we were serving. What they modeled was not obligation-driven service, but love-shaped formation.

After we transitioned out of that ministry, my husband and I joined another church community. We intentionally sat for a season, observing and discerning how God wanted us to move in that space. I served briefly on the praise and worship team, but eventually, I found myself drawn back into children's ministry. Honestly, it wasn't what I wanted—but it was where God needed me. So, I surrendered to the Father and served with a joyful heart. Love often leads us into places we wouldn't choose for ourselves, not to burden us, but to shape us.

In ministry, God's love often guides us into spaces we didn't envision for ourselves. Eventually, Marlon and I were invited to help with the marriage ministry. One of the greatest lessons I learned in that season was this: you can't lead in love in an area of ministry if you're not living that love out in your own life. God had to work in us first—refining our own marriage—so that we could serve others with integrity and compassion. Ministry does not form love; love forms ministry.

God is Love

After about six years, we began to feel a stirring to move on. We didn't know where we were headed—until we met a wonderful couple who would play a key role in our next chapter. When I reflect on the journey of serving in ministry, I'm reminded of how God often uses unexpected moments and connections to place us exactly where we need to be. My husband first encountered Pastors James and Denise while visiting their ministry with a close friend. He enjoyed the experience, but at the time, we were still committed to another church community. Sometime later, this couple was invited to a fellowship gathering at our home. I was meeting them for the first time that day. What stood out to me immediately wasn't their title or position—it was their humility. They didn't come announcing who they were or expecting to be treated a certain way. They showed up simply as guests.

I'll never forget how Pastor Jim walked into our house and started helping, unprompted. That moment caught me off guard in the best way. Here was someone I had never met before—a pastor—jumping right in without any sense of superiority or need to be honored. Both he and Pastor Denise blended in like they had always been part of our lives, sharing in laughter and fellowship with sincerity and joy. That kind of service cannot be manufactured; it only flows from love that has already been formed.

At that point, I still hadn't visited their church, but when my husband had to undergo surgery for gallstones shortly afterward, I called them—and they came. They weren't our pastors, yet they responded like shepherds. Pastor Jim showed up to the hospital every day to visit Marlon and brought me food. Pastor Denise was just as present, making sure we were supported. Our then-pastor, Pastor Mark, also came to see us. That entire experience was a beautiful picture of the Kingdom—no competition, no ego—just love and unity in action.

After Marlon was discharged, Pastors Jim and Denise brought food to our home so I wouldn't have to worry about cooking for the kids. That kind of service left a mark on my heart. We eventually transitioned to their ministry not because we were leaving a bad situation, but because we sensed God moving us forward. About six months later, our previous ministry closed, and Pastor Mark stepped into the next phase of his calling. Looking back, I see how God was moving all of us in His timing.

Once we joined our new church family, we were able to settle in and begin serving again. Within a few months, I was back in ministry, and eventually, my husband and I became leaders over the marriage ministry. Serving felt natural—it was part of who we were. But even in the familiarity of ministry, the enemy tried to creep in. He attempted to sow seeds of offense, doubt, and discontentment in my heart, using my own flaws and wounds to pull me away from the place where God had planted me. Obligation breeds resentment, but love invites endurance.

Still, God's voice was louder than the lies. His Spirit gently urged me to stay. I'm so thankful I listened. The longer I remained, the more I began to see His love—not just in sermons, but in the lives of my leaders and the people we fellowship with. This church community isn't just a building or a Sunday routine. It's family. Here, we haven't just received love—we've been taught how to love, and how to serve from that love rather than for it.

Serving in ministry is not always easy. Sometimes it requires sacrifice, humility, and patience. It means working with people who are different from you, forgiving offenses, and laying down your preferences for the good of others. But this is what Jesus demonstrated for us. Mark 10:45 tells us that "the Son of Man did not come to be served, but to serve." His service flowed from who He was, not from what He needed to prove.

When we serve from a place of love, everything changes. We don't serve to be seen, but because we begin to see others through God's eyes. We don't quit when we're overlooked, because our service is unto the Lord. We forgive quickly, because love keeps no record of wrongs. And we honor leadership—not because they are perfect—but because love governs our posture, not obligation.

Ministry becomes burdensome when it flows from expectation. But when it flows from God's love, it becomes a joy. Galatians 5:13 reminds us that we are called to freedom, and that freedom expresses itself through serving one another in love. Love is not proven by attendance, visibility, or how often we say yes. Love is formed in us and expressed through us.

I'm a strong believer in exercising my freedom in Christ to say no—especially when something isn't a clear directive from God. Love does not erase boundaries, but it does sometimes call us to stretch beyond convenience. When I say yes now, it is not out of pressure, but out of care.

I am grateful for every lesson God has taught me in ministry. I am grateful for leaders who modeled servant leadership. I am grateful for a spiritual family that has shown me what it means to be the hands and feet of Jesus. And above all, I am grateful for God's love that continues to teach me how to serve with a right heart—because love is not something we prove, it is something that forms us and then flows through us.

Father, thank You for the example of servant-hearted leaders who reflect Your love through their actions. Thank You for placing in me a heart to serve—not out of obligation, but out of love. Help me to be led by love, even when it calls me beyond my comfort zone. Teach me to serve with joy, with compassion, and with the desire to reflect who You are. Remind me that love is not about pressure, but about Your Spirit working through me. May every act of service be a reflection of You, and a demonstration of Your heart. In Jesus' name, amen.

Chapter 9

Love in the Workplace

I believe that our workplaces are often the mission fields where God calls us to demonstrate His love in practical ways. Whether we are leading a team, serving customers, or simply working alongside colleagues, how we reflect God's love can impact lives and open doors for His Kingdom.

I haven't worked in a traditional workplace in years, but I still remember clearly the places and seasons where God taught me valuable lessons about loving others at work.

One of the most defining moments was early after I returned to serving God. I was working as a typesetter, and a promotion opportunity opened when my manager was leaving. Initially, my manager guaranteed me the promotion. However, a young woman who had previously worked there returned and rekindled a relationship with my manager. Because of that, I was passed over for the promotion. I was angry and hurt.

I confided in a woman of God named Valerie Rose who also worked there. She knew my heart was a mess, but she faithfully prayed for me. Valerie was one of the first people I told when I came back to the Lord, and her prayers were powerful. I remember telling her how much I hated that young woman. Valerie ministered to me, praying over me and helping me see beyond my anger.

After my manager left, the young woman became my manager. I had to work with her daily, and at first, it was difficult. But one day, when she came to me about something, God suddenly gave me a wave of compassion for her. I sensed a deep hurt inside her that had nothing to do with me. She was simply lashing out because of her own insecurities and hurts. I excused myself to the bathroom and cried—not from anger, but from a heart moved by God's love.

From that moment on, God taught me to treat her with love, regardless of how she treated me. Eventually, I was fired over someone else's lie. But because God's love had softened my heart, I did not leave bitter. Instead, I left with peace and gratitude for the lessons God was teaching me. However, I was mad because they let me work an entire day, told me I was fired, and escorted me out the back door. I can laugh today. Thank God His love in me did not allow me to stay angry.

Later, I worked for a toner cartridge company surrounded by a diverse group of people, some wealthy, some not. My boss trusted me immensely, even allowing me to care for her two young sons, stay in her home and drive her vehicle while she was on business trips. I believe she saw the love of God in me reflected through my actions and attitude based on the fact that she told me I was the only one on the job that she could trust with her kids. On this same job, I met a supervisor from the California office who was an atheist. Despite knowing his unbelief, I treated him with kindness and respect. He was astonished by my genuine love and friendliness. He literally came to me and said, "I don't understand … you are being nice to me even though I don't believe there is a God." It was a testimony that God's love transcends beliefs and touches hearts in unexpected ways. Be careful not to shun people just because they don't believe what you believe.

I once worked for a company where both my supervisor and a coworker professed to be believers. I truly thought we were all getting along well. But one day, I was unexpectedly given two weeks' notice and was told it was because I had been speaking negatively about the company. That was not true. I suspected my coworker may have been involved, especially after noticing she had been called into the boss's office shortly before it happened. I was deeply hurt and angry about being let go. But the Lord began to work in my heart. He led me to do something that I would never have done on my own. He put it on my heart to buy my supervisor a thank-you card for training me on the job. He also prompted me to send an email to the owner of the company, expressing my gratitude for the opportunity to work and learn there. God didn't stop there. He led me to purchase an expensive bottle of perfume for the coworker who had sold me out. I had complimented her on it once, and she told me she had bought it for herself because no one would ever give her something that costly. God remembered that moment, and He moved through me to be the one to do it. I could have walked away bitter, but the love of God wouldn't let me.

After being fired, the next week the Lord led me to an amazing temp job in corporate America for a mortgage banking company. At first, I questioned why God had placed me there, but He revealed that while the people there had natural talents and skills, they needed to know Him. I was carrying His presence into that space. Being the only woman in the office, I experienced respect from my male coworkers because God enabled me to serve them in love. I made it clear that my family was my priority, and they honored that boundary. This mutual respect created a healthy work environment where love was evident. That temp job became a salaried position for the next 10 years until I chose to become a stay-at-home mom.

Finally, after both of my sons were school age, I worked at my children's private Christian school. Many assume working in a Christian school is easy when it comes to love, but children—whether in Christian or secular environments—can challenge you. The blessing was that I could discipline using Scripture and the Spirit's leading without fear of governmental interference. It was a sacred place to demonstrate the love of God in correction and encouragement.

Now, I own my own business serving veterans. They come to me with physical injuries, mental health struggles, and emotional pain. It takes the love of God to do more than just handle claims. I must hear their hearts, minister compassion, and meet their needs beyond paperwork. Sometimes I have to pray with them. That kind of ministry flows only from a heart transformed by God's love.

Showing God's love in the workplace means going beyond mere professionalism or politeness. It means embodying the character of Christ in everything you do. It looks like patience when coworkers are difficult or situations become frustrating. It shows up as kindness in your words, even when others aren't kind in return. It's reflected in humility—choosing not to boast or elevate yourself above others. It includes forgiveness when you've been wronged, refusing to let grudges poison the atmosphere around you. It means walking in integrity, doing what's right even when no one is watching. And it expresses itself through generosity—whether with your time, encouragement, or resources. Serving in the workplace is not about a title or task but about revealing God's heart through how you show up each day.

The workplace is often marked by competition, politics, pressure, and stress. It can be a space where people feel overlooked, undervalued, or drained. Yet for the believer, it is also a powerful mission field. When we choose to love as God loves—even in high-stress environments—we become His representatives. We reflect His nature not just in what we say, but in how we carry ourselves, treat others, and handle conflict.

In Matthew 5:13–16, Jesus says to His disciples, "You are the salt of the earth… You are the light of the world. A town built on a hill cannot be hidden." This is more than a poetic metaphor—it's a divine calling. Salt, in the ancient world, was used to preserve food from decay and rot. Spiritually, Jesus is calling His followers to live in such a way that they preserve righteousness, truth, and integrity in a world prone to moral decay. In the workplace, this means we stand against gossip, dishonesty, and corruption—not always through confrontation, but often through quiet consistency, integrity, and love. When others cut corners, we work with excellence. When people tear others down, we build them up. We preserve godly values by living them out daily.

Jesus also calls us the light of the world—not because of our own light, but because of His light shining through us. He continues in Matthew 5:16, "Let your light so shine before others, that they may see your good works and glorify your Father in heaven." In practical terms, this means our kindness, patience, honesty, and grace in the workplace are not just personality traits—they are reflections of God's love. The workplace may be filled with darkness—unethical practices, manipulation, pride—but when we walk in and choose love over competition, gentleness over aggression, and truth over flattery, we shine. The love of God becomes visible through our choices and conduct.

Showing God's love at work doesn't always mean quoting Scripture or preaching during lunch breaks. Sometimes, it's letting someone else take credit without bitterness. It's forgiving a coworker who wronged you, helping a struggling teammate, or choosing not to participate in office gossip. These seemingly small acts become spiritual markers that distinguish us in a dark world.

Colossians 3:23-24 reminds us, "Whatever you do, work at it with all your heart, as working for the Lord, not for human masters, since you know that you will receive an inheritance from the Lord as a reward. It is the Lord Christ you are serving." 1 Corinthians 16:14 says,

God is Love

"Do everything in love." These perspectives transform our attitude. Work is no longer just a job or a means to an end. It becomes an act of worship, a ministry opportunity, and a way to bring God's love into the everyday.

As you go into your workplace—whether as an employee, employer, volunteer, or business owner—remember that your role is to represent Christ's love. You may not always be able to share words about Jesus openly, but your love actions will speak volumes.

Father, thank You for every opportunity to demonstrate Your love—whether I'm working for someone else or for myself. Thank You for helping me to forgive when I'm wronged, just as You have so graciously forgiven me. Teach me to serve with a willing heart, not just work for a paycheck. Help me to work as unto You and not unto man, with excellence and integrity that reflects who You are. May my efforts never be for personal recognition, but always to bring You glory. Let my work be a witness of Your love at all times. In Jesus' name, amen.

Latonya Sterling

Chapter 10

Love and Leadership

Leadership is more than holding a title or giving direction. It is not rooted in visibility, control, or personal influence. True leadership in the Kingdom of God flows from Christ at work within us. Any responsibility we are given—to lead a ministry, guide a team, parent at home, or serve in the community—is not an identity we take on, but a role we steward. As believers, we do not lead from ourselves; we lead from the love of Christ already formed in us.

To lead, then, is not to manufacture an atmosphere by our own strength, but to follow Christ faithfully in the specific responsibility entrusted to us. Jesus does not call us to dominate or manage people, but to serve them in love. He said that whoever desires to be great must become a servant (Matthew 20:26–28). Leadership is not about imposing personal preferences, silent expectations, or control. It is about clearly communicating, serving with humility, and allowing the love of Christ to shape how we guide others. Love must already be evident in a person's life before leadership is entrusted to them, because love—not position—is what truly leads.

The Holy Spirit leads us with gentleness. He does not manipulate or control but guides us into truth with patience and grace (John 16:13). If God Himself leads His people this way, then those of us who are entrusted to lead others must follow His example. We lead not by lording over others, but by coming alongside them, empowering them, and loving them through every challenge.

The Bible gives us both warnings and encouragement when it comes to leadership. One example of failed leadership can be seen in the story of Rehoboam, Solomon's son. When Rehoboam became king, the people came to him asking for relief from the heavy burden his father had placed on them. The elders advised Rehoboam to speak kindly to the people and lighten their load, promising that if he did, they would serve him loyally. But instead, he rejected their counsel and took the advice of his peers, telling the people, "My father disciplined you with whips, but I will discipline you with scorpions" (1 Kings 12:14). His harshness and lack of compassion caused a division among the people and ultimately led to the kingdom being torn apart (1 Kings 12:1–20). Rehoboam's story is a reminder that leadership without love breeds rebellion, resentment, and ruin.

But there are also beautiful examples of what loving leadership looks like. Nehemiah was a cupbearer to the king, but God gave him a burden to rebuild the broken walls of Jerusalem. His leadership was marked by prayer, humility, compassion, and strength. He didn't just supervise from a distance; he rolled up his sleeves and worked alongside the people. When the people were afraid, he encouraged them. When there was injustice, he confronted it. When opposition came, he prayed. His leadership was effective because it was rooted in love—for God and for the people (Nehemiah 1–6). As a result, the walls were rebuilt, and the people were united and restored.

God is Love

I began to learn the power of loving leadership at a young age. At 19 years old, I was promoted to a management position at Hardee's. I was young, but I could already see how some in leadership positions treated employees with disrespect and insensitivity. It bothered me. I knew there had to be a better way. So, I chose to lead differently. I encouraged my team, worked alongside them, and made sure they felt seen and appreciated. What I noticed was that when people feel valued, they work harder, trust more, and take pride in their work. That's the fruit of leading with love.

Even when we lead with love, we can still get hurt. It's one of the hardest parts of leadership. You can do everything with the right heart—serve faithfully, speak kindly, support others—and still face criticism, betrayal, or rejection. Sometimes the very people you pour into will walk away, gossip, or misunderstand you. This can be especially painful for those of us who take leadership as a calling from God. More pastors, than most people realize, are hurt by the very people they serve. It may feel unfair. It may tempt those who are hurt to retreat or shut down. Yet, this is where the love of Christ sustains us. Jesus, the perfect leader, was rejected, mocked, and abandoned by those He came to save. And yet, He never stopped loving. He never stopped leading. He forgave from the cross and kept entrusting Himself to the Father (Hebrews 12:3).

When individuals in leadership are hurt, Jesus is the Savior who understands. His love is not only our example, but it is our healing balm. Through His love, we find the strength to forgive, to stay tender, and to continue leading even when it hurts.

Leadership is not about perfection. It's about being faithful. It's about leading in a way that points people to God, not to ourselves. It's about using our influence to build up, not tear down. It's about staying rooted in love, even when it's difficult, because love is what truly transforms people and environments.

In every arena—whether the pulpit or the breakroom, the boardroom or the dining room—God calls us to lead with love. And when we do, His presence goes before us, His grace sustains us, and His power works through us. We may be hurt along the way, but we will not be overcome. For love—true, godly love—never fails (Romans 2:4).

Father, thank You for the sacred call to lead. Teach me to lead like Jesus—with humility, compassion, and grace. When I'm tempted to control, remind me of Your gentleness. When I face rejection or hurt, anchor me in Your healing love. Let my leadership reflect Your heart and not my ego. Help me to serve with joy, to speak with wisdom, and to love with endurance. May those I lead see You in me. Strengthen me to lead faithfully, even when it's hard, and let love always be my motivation. In Jesus' name, amen.

Chapter 11

Love that Corrects

God's love is not rainbows and unicorns. It's not some sentimental feeling that overlooks our behavior or winks at sin. The love of God is holy, righteous and just. It is fierce in its pursuit of our good, even when that good requires correction. There is a dangerous misconception circulating in today's world that because God is love, we can live however we want, and His love will simply cover us. While His love is indeed powerful and immeasurable, it is not permissive to live a lifestyle of sin. Out of God's love flows discipline. Hebrews 12:6 tells us clearly, "The Lord disciplines the one he loves, and he chastens everyone he accepts as his son." Discipline is not the opposite of love—it is a powerful expression of it.

We don't serve a God who loves us to the point that sin becomes acceptable. Sin is *never* acceptable to God, and His love does not change that. Love does not ignore truth; it partners with it. People often ask, "If God is love, how can He send people to hell?" The truth is, God doesn't send people to hell. People make that choice themselves by rejecting the only way of salvation—Jesus Christ. It is not God's will for anyone to perish (2 Peter 3:9); in fact, He made the ultimate sacrifice so that no one would have to be eternally separated from Him. The greatest demonstration of God's love was sending His only begotten Son to die in our place, to offer eternal life to all who believe. To accuse God of sending people to hell is to disregard the greatness of His mercy and the gift of choice He has given us. God doesn't force separation from Himself; rather, when we refuse His mercy and reject His love, we choose separation, hell, for ourselves.

Throughout Scripture, we see countless examples of God's love through correction. Israel, His chosen people, repeatedly disobeyed and turned to idols, yet God never stopped loving them. He disciplined them—sometimes through captivity, famine, or silence—not because He hated them, but because He longed for them to return to Him. His correction was never without purpose. It was always aimed at restoration. Even in His discipline, God remained faithful, merciful, and loving.

Peter also offers a personal glimpse into this side of God's love. When Peter impulsively cut off the ear of the soldier at Jesus' arrest, Jesus immediately corrected him, saying, "Put your sword back in its place" (Matthew 26:52). And even more telling, when Peter later denied Jesus three times, Jesus didn't reject him. Instead, after the resurrection, Jesus sought Peter out personally. He restored him, reaffirmed his calling, and instructed him to feed His sheep. This was not love that excused wrong. It was love that corrected, healed, and empowered Peter to walk in truth and purpose.

The love of God is not the absence of discipline. In fact, *discipline is one of the greatest forms of love*. It is not a punishment driven by God's anger, but training and instruction from a loving Father who sees beyond the moment. God's discipline is designed to steer us away from destructive patterns, to protect our minds, our hearts, and even our physical lives. His correction is not to shame us, but to save us. Just as a parent disciplines a child to keep them from danger, Father lovingly steps in to align us with His truth so we may walk in freedom and wholeness. This isn't freedom to live ungodly. It's freedom to know Father. It's freedom to receive God's love and reciprocate it to others and to God through obedience. This is a freedom to honor God and reflect His character in the earth.

We don't have to figure things out on our own. Our Father has given us the Holy Spirit to help us. In John 16:8, Jesus speaks of the Spirit's role in bringing conviction. However, many have misunderstood this verse to mean that the Holy Spirit convicts *believers* of sin. A closer look reveals that this passage actually refers to the Spirit convicting *the world*—not believers—of sin, righteousness, and judgment. Verse 9 clarifies that the specific sin mentioned is unbelief in Jesus.

There are some in the church, *not all*, who interpret the word "convict" as a deep awareness of wrongdoing, often accompanied by guilt that leads to a change in behavior. The problem is that guilt doesn't change the heart. The Greek word used in John 16:8 is *elenchō*, which means to expose, refute, or bring to light with the goal of convincing or correcting. It carries the idea of presenting truth in such a way that it reveals error and calls for acknowledgment—not to condemn, but to lead to clarity and change. This is all for the purpose of Holy Spirit to lovingly draw the unbeliever to Jesus Christ.

The word *elenchō* doesn't imply condemnation for those who are in Christ. In fact, Scripture is clear in Romans 8:1: There is now no condemnation for those who are in Christ Jesus. Instead, His role in the life of a believer is far more restorative. The Holy Spirit is not sent to shame or condemn us, but to teach, guide, correct, and remind us of our righteousness in Christ. He lovingly leads us into truth (John 16:13), affirms our identity as God's children (Romans 8:16), and shows us how to walk in alignment with who we are in Him (Gal 5:16).

Everything God does flows from the heart of a good Father—not a harsh judge—and that includes how He relates to both the lost and the found. We were once lost, but Love found us.

The next time you feel the correction of Father or experience His discipline, don't run from it. Don't confuse it with rejection or anger. Recognize it for what it is: *Love*. It is proof that you are His. It is proof that He loves you too much to let you destroy yourself. The love of God is more than a feeling—it is God Himself shaping us, transforming us, and keeping us on the path of life.

Father, thank You for loving me so much that You sent Your only Son, Jesus, to make a way for me to know You. Thank You for Your loving discipline that protects me, shapes me, and draws me closer to Your heart. Help me to welcome Your correction, knowing it comes from a place of deep love. Continue to work in me, Lord—give me a heart that desires to please You, not out of fear or obligation, but because I recognize and am moved by Your unfailing love for me. In Jesus' name, amen.

Final Word: The Love That Never Ends

We began this journey with a simple yet profound truth: **God is love**. We've explored what that means—not as a concept, but as a living, transforming reality. We've looked at what love is, how to know God's love for ourselves, and how to release that love to others. And yet, even with all we've uncovered, we've only begun to scratch the surface. His love is deeper than the ocean, wider than the horizon, and higher than the heavens. It is a love no human mind can fully comprehend without the revelation of the Holy Spirit.

Paul writes in Romans 8:38–39, "For I am convinced that neither death nor life, neither angels nor demons, neither the present nor the future, nor any powers, neither height nor depth, nor anything else in all creation, will be able to separate us from the love of God that is in Christ Jesus our Lord." That means nothing—not your past, not your present struggles, not your future mistakes—can separate you from His love. His love is not conditional, fragile, or fleeting. It is strong. Unshakable. Eternal. And this love doesn't just comfort—it transforms. It changes how we see ourselves, how we relate to others, and how we live, serve, and grow. This journey has never been about rules, routines, or religious performance. It's been about learning to live from a place of intimacy with God—a place where His love leads, corrects, strengthens, and heals. It starts in the heart.

I've shared moments of joy and pain, of struggle and breakthrough—not as someone who has arrived, but as someone still being shaped by the love of a perfect Father. I'm still learning that love isn't always convenient or comfortable. Sometimes it calls us to stay when we'd rather leave, to forgive when we want to hold on, to serve quietly when no one is watching, and to say yes when it costs us something. Sometimes love means saying no—setting boundaries, walking in wisdom, and guarding our hearts from bitterness and burnout. Even then, love is still leading.

Love doesn't start with us. It begins with Him. "We love because He first loved us" (1 John 4:19). Because of that truth, we can love and live freely—unafraid to give, to serve, to submit, to forgive, to speak truth, and to be led by the Spirit rather than by emotions or expectations. That is the freedom found in knowing that love isn't just what God does—it's who He is. And, it is demonstrated through action, not merely words that are spoken to make someone feel good.

So, wherever you are in your journey, stay rooted in His love. Let it define you, guide you, and overflow from you. Let it be your motivation, your anchor, and your response—whether you're on the mountaintop or in the valley. Never settle for simply knowing about God's love; live in it. Experience it daily. Walk in it intentionally. And let it be evident in every relationship and every assignment He entrusts to you.

This is not the end. This is a beginning—a beginning of deeper love, deeper grace, and deeper freedom in Christ. May your life echo this unshakable truth: God is love—and His love in you is more than enough.

Closing Prayer

A Prayer to Live in God's Love

Father God,
Thank You for loving me with a love that is beyond my understanding. Thank You for pursuing me, choosing me, and calling me Your own—not because of what I've done, but because of who You are. You are love, and in You, I am safe, seen, and secure.

Lord, I don't want to just know about Your love—I want to live in it. Help me to be fully yielded to Your presence. Heal what is broken, soften what has grown hard, and awaken what has gone numb. Let Your love correct me without crushing me, lead me without pressuring me, and strengthen me without striving.

I surrender the lies I've believed about who I am and who You are. I release the fear, the shame, and the need to earn what You've already freely given. Teach me to receive Your love without resistance and to reflect it without reservation.

Help me to love others with the same grace and truth You extend to me. Whether it's in my home, my relationships, my calling, or my daily interactions—cause Your love flow through me that it may be my motivation, my foundation, and my response.

Holy Spirit, guide me. When I'm tempted to perform for approval or hide in fear, remind me that I am fully accepted in Jesus. When I feel weak, remind me that Your love is my strength. When I'm unsure, help me to trust that love never fails—because You never fail.

Today, I choose to live loved. Not because I feel it every moment, but because I believe what You've said: nothing can separate me from Your love. Form this truth in me until it becomes my identity, my peace, and my purpose.

In Jesus' name, amen

Works Cited

Encyclopaedia Britannica. *Plato*. Encyclopaedia Britannica, 2024, https://www.britannica.com/biography/Plato. Accessed 15 July 2025.

Encyclopaedia Britannica. *Aristotle*. Encyclopaedia Britannica, 2024, https://www.britannica.com/biography/Aristotle. Accessed 15 July 2025.

Holy Bible, New International Version®, NIV®. Copyright ©1973, 1978, 1984, 2011 by Biblica, Inc.™

PREVIOUS WORK

Latonya L. Simmons Sterling

The Beginning of My Beginning
Freedom: From Religious Rituals to Intimacy with God

Explore the journey from religious bondage to a personal, transformative relationship with God. This book invites readers into a deeper intimacy with God, embracing freedom through grace and love.

COMING SOON

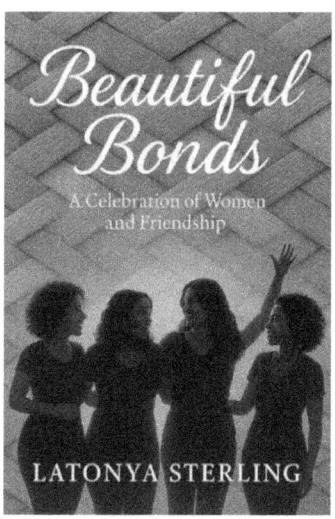

Beautiful Bonds is a heartfelt celebration of the power of strong, godly friendships between women. Through personal stories and reflections, Latonya Sterling honors the women who have walked beside her, challenged her, inspired her, and loved her through every season. From laughter to tears, prayers to breakthroughs, these relationships reveal how true friendship—rooted in love, trust, and faith—can shape who we become. *Beautiful Bonds* reminds us that sisterhood is not just a blessing; it's a reflection of God's heart for connection, encouragement, and shared strength.

SUGGESTED READING

In *Divine Love*, Apostle Larry Herring unpacks the transforming power of God's Spirit and grace, showing how His perfect love casts out fear and breaks the chains of guilt and performance. Rooted in Romans 8 and Luke 4:18, this book guides readers into freedom, healing, and the embrace of God's unfailing love. With honesty and Spirit-filled wisdom, Apostle Herring invites believers to live as God's beloved children, walking in identity and liberty.

www.ingramcontent.com/pod-product-compliance
Lightning Source LLC
Chambersburg PA
CBHW020019050426
42450CB00005B/549